THE GOLF SWING
OF THE FUTURE

THE
GOLF SWING OF
THE FUTURE

MINDY BLAKE, D.S.O., D.F.C., M.Sc

W·W·NORTON & COMPANY·INC·*New York*

First American edition 1973

Library of Congress Cataloging in Publication Data

Blake, Mindy.
  The golf swing of the future.

  1. Swing (Golf)   I. Title.
GV979.S9B52   1973   796.352'3   73–400
ISBN 0–393–08376–4

PRINTED IN THE UNITED STATES OF AMERICA

1   2   3   4   5   6   7   8   9   0

CONTENTS

Illustrated by COLIN REID

INTRODUCTION

During a friendly round with Mindy Blake at Wentworth, Ed Sullivan, the American TV showman,
found himself experiencing one of those days which
impel golfers to hurl clubs and trolley into the nearest
pond and stomp off to the clubhouse, vowing never
to set foot on tee again. "I wonder," suggested
Mindy, "if you would like to try a different method."
Ed Sullivan said despairingly that he would gladly
try anything. He listened carefully, stepped up to the
ball—and proceeded to belt it out of sight. To his
surprise and gratification, for the remainder of the
round he continued to play golf such as he had never
played before, and, when they came off the 18th, he
went straight to the pro.'s shop, bought the entire
stock of golf balls and made Mindy a present of
them.

This story came to my ears in the autumn of 1968
and I thought it would make an interesting item for
a column called "Sports and Sportsmen" which I was
contributing at the time to the London *Observer*. I
drove down to see Mindy at his Surrey home and, in
the natural course of things, asked what golden
principles he had imparted to his American guest.
This book is an expanded version of his answer. I
helped him to get it down on paper because he is a
busy man with plenty of things (including playing
golf) to occupy him, but all the ideas are solely his.
They add a new chapter—or, rather, several new
chapters—to an already extraordinary life.

Mindy Blake is the son of a New Zealand country
schoolmaster who, in order to send his son to

university, mortgaged his salary to buy a small chicken farm where Mindy could live and also make some money while a student. For four years, between lectures and books, he hatched chicks, milked his cow and cooked for himself. At the end of that time he had an honours degree in mathematics and a job as physics lecturer at his university. He was also recognised as the leading gymnast in New Zealand; he had, furthermore, won the New Zealand pole vault championship with a new record height only nine months after taking up the sport as second string for his college; and, when his country introduced compulsory egg grading, he had begun his career as an inventor by coming up with an automatic egg-weighing machine which was to be used until long after the end of World War II.

In 1936 he came to Britain and joined the R.A.F. He was R.A.F. pole vault champion from 1937 to 1939 and from 1946 to 1948. The intervening period was taken up by the war, during which he was credited with shooting down ten enemy aircraft, won the D.S.O. and D.F.C. and bore what is technically known as a charmed life. He became, by accident rather than design, the first man to land a Hurricane fighter upside down in the foundations of a hospital, and, by design rather than accident, the first pilot to ditch a Spitfire in the sea and survive, and also the first pilot to bale out of a Spitfire at an altitude of 200 ft and live to explain how it was done.

The episode with the Hurricane happened during a night-flying exercise on September 8, 1939, five days after the outbreak of war. His squadron was based at Croydon, a grass airfield, and, with nobody very clear about what immediate course the hostilities would take, the aircraft were parked in the open and the pilots slept under the wings. When they switched the flares on for a few seconds as Mindy came in to land, he realised he was going to overshoot and opened up his throttle to go round again. His engine promptly stopped. At 300 ft in pitch darkness he had no alternative but to tighten his straps, slow to stalling speed and wait to see what happened. What happened was that the Hurricane hit the chimney of a nurses' home, flipped over in the air and fell into the foundations of the new Purley hospital. Mindy stepped out of the wreckage unhurt apart from a head cut which required eighteen stitches, and he was flying again within a few days. Hurricanes had never been parked out in the open before and the cause of the crash was subsequently established as hay in the air intake, a verdict which seems appropriate to those unreal and early days of "the phoney war".

The second incident occurred around 9 a.m. on an August morning in 1941 when Mindy's Spitfire was shot up over Cherbourg. Over the radio he told the rest of his wing: "I've got a bullet in the cooling system. I reckon I have nine minutes before the engine seizes up. When you get back tell them I'm putting down in the sea about seven miles off the coast." They said: "Bale out." "No," he said. "I think I can manage it."

At that time nobody had ditched a Spitfire in the sea and come out alive. The problems involved, however, had been exercising Mindy's mind for some time, particularly since he had seen Paddy Finucane, the legendary Irish ace, disappear for ever beneath the Channel waves. He had worked out that the retarding force applied to a pilot's body when a Spitfire hit the water and stopped was from five to seven Gs, which meant you were either killed instantly or you were rendered unconscious and drowned. He had also hit upon a method which he was confident would

9

reduce the G-force to around one-and-a-half, thus giving a pilot a reasonable chance of survival.

Seven miles off the coast, just as his Spitfire was about to hit the water, he tilted one wing-tip deliberately into the sea and cartwheeled the aircraft. A few minutes later he was safely in his inflatable dinghy and paddling for the English coast. With the aid of a following wind, he had already made more than five miles when search aircraft passed overhead an hour later on their way to look for him. They searched all day without success, constantly droning through the sky over his head. He was finally picked up twelve hours after the ditching, by which time he had paddled to within two miles of the Isle of Wight.

In 1942 Mindy invented the R.A.F.'s first fighter gyro gunsight, which allowed automatically for deflection and was used successfully throughout the war. He made an instruction film on its use and, as a climax, set off on the 1942 Dieppe raid to shoot down an enemy fighter. He succeeded—but a few seconds later, at only 200 ft above the sea, was himself the victim of an attack. A cannonshell shattered his windshield at point-blank range, blinding him with Perspex.

He had also been aware of the possibility of finding himself in this predicament and had decided that, should it happen, there was only one real hope of escape—to slide back the cockpit cover, undo your straps, sit back in your seat, put your foot on the control column and send the plane diving straight into the sea. In the course of this manoeuvre he judged a pilot would be shot out of his cockpit like a stone from a catapult and gain valuable extra feet in height.

He proved quite correct. He described a graceful parabola through the air, his parachute opened a split second before he hit the water, and, within a few minutes, he had his K-type dinghy inflated and was paddling again. He paddled all day, all night and most of the next day although able to squint out of one eye for only a painful fraction of a second at a time. Five miles from Dover he was picked up by a German launch.

After he had spent three weeks in hospital outside Paris, it was decided to take him to Frankfurt for interrogation. He started the journey in a car with a driver, a sergeant and a German officer. At a lonely spot between the hospital and Paris, the car stopped and all three Germans got out and disappeared. Mindy's instinct told him to make a run for it: his head told him to stay where he was. Eventually the Germans returned and, on the train later, the officer revealed that he had represented his country in the 400 metres at the 1936 Olympics. "So you hoped I would make a dash for it back there in the car," said Mindy. "Yes," said the officer, "it would have made good headlines for me."

The disposition of German troops in France was fairly well-known at that time. Mindy was aware that, about 40 miles out of Paris, the train would be passing through a region where the Wehrmacht was thin on the ground and where there would be several steep gradients. He pretended to have an upset stomach and, an hour-and-a-half out of Paris, when the German officer escorting him had dozed off, he set out on his third and final visit to the lavatory at the end of the corridor.

He put his boot through the window, wrapped his head in his tunic, climbed out and hung by one hand to get his feet going for the drop. He was just about to let go when he realised by a change in the sound of the wheels that the train had started to cross a viaduct. Although weakened by the morphine given to him in the course of treating his eyes, he managed to hang on until the train had crossed the river. Then he just had to let go.

In the resulting fall he broke one hand and was severely cut about the head. At the time, British pilots were under instructions to report to a French farmhouse at dawn if shot down, and as many as twenty were getting safely back to Britain each week. But Mindy was unable to find a farmhouse and was delayed in his search by jumping over a wall and landing in a thick bramble bush where, in his enfeebled state, he was trapped for several hours.

It was well past dawn by the time he extricated himself and he settled down to wait until first light next morning. As the hours passed he decided he could no longer stand the pain, the loss of blood, the heat and the flies. He set off in broad daylight and eventually found a farm. The farmer summoned a vet. to deal with his injuries. Shortly afterwards, however, the village postman arrived and said: "Everyone in the village knows a British pilot is sheltering here." The farmer, who had several children, decided the risk was too great. He rang up the Germans.

Later, in Frankfurt, Mindy explained: "If the officer escorting me falls asleep, you must expect me to try to escape"—and he had the pleasure of seeing the officer in question arrested. It served him right, he still feels, for the trick he tried to play on him in the car between the hospital and Paris. Mindy spent the rest of the war in a prison camp where, in part, he occupied himself by designing a new kind of rotary engine.

His ambition was always "to have a workshop at the bottom of the garden and invent things". Today he has just that. His inventions include a golf club which enables the dedicated player to practise effectively in his own drawing-room, a supersonic aircraft which is on the secret list, another rotary engine and a car seat belt which promises to be at least 50 per cent cheaper than anything else on the market. Most of his spare time is taken up with thinking about golf, talking about golf and playing golf at Wentworth, which is just a good drive and several fairway woods from his home.

"To understand golf," he says, "you need the kind of mind which is good at mathematics and physics. Golf is purely a matter of technique"—like cartwheeling Spitfires and baling out of them successfully at 200 ft.

Harry Weaver

THE TROUBLE WITH GOLF

Study of the basic technique involved in hitting a golf ball efficiently, cleanly and accurately is still only in its infancy. I begin with this challenging statement because it is my reason for adding to the dozens of volumes about golf which already grace the bookshelves. It is, I believe, the lack of a basic technique, scientifically and athletically sound, which accounts for the confusion and uncertainty that exist even at the highest level of this, the most difficult of all games. The degree of that confusion and uncertainty can be easily demonstrated. Just consider the following points.

Top pros, differ fundamentally from each other in the way they hit the ball, and, in writing about the game, offer contradictory advice on the "correct" way of playing it.

Tommy Armour, for instance, says the chip shot is a short jab with a crisp hit with the hands. Gay Brewer, on the other hand, describes the chip shot as a drag movement: he senses that the back of his left hand pushes the club back straight and drags it down through the ball.

Sam Snead says that one of the hacker's most common and widespread faults is raising his right elbow away from the body during the backswing. This must make Jack Nicklaus the most distinguished hacker in the history of golf: he does just that.

Henry Cotton advocates hitting against a braced left side. Jack Nicklaus and Arnold Palmer both have

15

the left knee bent at the moment of impact with the ball.

In the square-to-square method, recognised as the most modern technique, a weak position of the left thumb (i.e. on top of the shaft) is recommended. Yet two of the top money winners, Billy Casper and Lee Trevino, both recognised as straight hitters, use a strong left thumb position behind the shaft (and, just to increase the confusion, Gary Player is "anti" the square-to-square method).

A highly controversial point is the position of the left wrist at the top of the swing and whether the clubface is open or shut. Leslie King, a leading British teacher, advocates an open clubface at the top of the swing. Most other teachers agree with him. Yet three of Britain's most successful pros., Dave Thomas, Brian Huggett and Neil Coles, all keep the clubface closed.

A comon pattern can be traced in the careers of the majority of top pros.—early brilliance, a number of years in the shadows, then success, often in their late thirties and early forties.

This pattern is, I believe, both highly significant and easily explained. In my view young players with natural flair for the game shoot to the top early in their career because co-ordination of hand and eye enables them to compensate for a basically faulty technique. This co-ordination, however, is one of the first gifts to disappear in a young athlete. If a golfer is made of the stuff of champions, he then has to go through years of dedicated practice and experiment until he eventually evolves an *individual* method which enables *him* to hit the ball consistently (and which is, incidentally, almost impossible to pass on to anyone else because of its individual nature).

16

The great Arnold Palmer provides a classic example. In *Arnold Palmer's Golf Book* he relates that he started fooling around with golf clubs at the age of three and, when only fourteen, shot a 71 in his first High School match. In his late 'teens and early twenties, however, when he decided to move his left hand over from the "hooker's grip" to the "weak" pro. position, he found himself all at sea.

He writes: "I had stopped hooking but was hitting everything to the right. I was smacking 1,000 or 1,500 golf balls off the practice tee every day and still was getting beaten week after week in tournaments."

He changed his grip in 1947. It was 1952 before "all of a sudden, the ball stopped going to the right and I was hanging shots straight as a string". For a superb athlete and talented player like Palmer to have to hit more than a quarter-of-a-million golf balls over a period of five years before "all of a sudden"—he gives no reason—they began to go straight suggests he was searching for a technique rather than building on a sound one which he already understood thoroughly.

In fact, he has had a thinnish time over the last few seasons. He has had a lot of difficulties with his game and, watching him at Wentworth during the 1968 and 1971 Piccadilly tournaments, it was clear that he is still questing for an elusive something which he feels is there. I feel sure we shall have to wait for his forties—as was the case with Ben Hogan, to choose one famous name at random—before we see him at the top again.

Despite their years of dedicated practice and experience, top pros. hit appalling shots from time to

*time. Even more significantly, it is not uncommon
for their game to desert them entirely.*

Leaving aside the occasional shockers—after all,
man is not a machine—it suggests that something
fundamental is lacking when an accepted master of a
sport loses his touch entirely and apparently has no
rational means of finding it again. Tournament
records provide plenty of examples.

In 1962, for example, Jack Nicklaus beat Arnold
Palmer by three strokes in an 18-hole play-off for the
U.S. Open. They then came to Troon for the British
Open. Palmer won with 276 (71, 69, 67, 69). Nicklaus
finished 29 shots behind him in 305. His rounds were
80, 72, 74, 79. After that opening 80 he said: "What
happened to me? I don't know. I'm all mixed up",
and retired in misery to the practice ground where,
on the basis of his next three rounds, he was able to
learn very little.

In the 1964 U.S. Open, the winner was Ken
Venturi. In the same tournament the following year
he failed to qualify for the final two rounds, returning
an 81 and a 79 to put himself 20 over par at the
halfway stage.

Jack Nicklaus had a similar experience in the 1967
U.S. Master, a tournament he had won for two suc-
cessive years. He chalked up a 72 and a 79 to become the first U.S. Masters titleholder in history not
to qualify for the final two rounds. His only comment
afterwards was: "Everything I did went wrong. My
luck deserted me." I think it might be argued that it
was his technique rather than his luck that went sour
on him. A 79 represents a remarkable deterioration
in the game of a player many, including myself, consider the finest golfer in the world today. Before anyone accuses me of anti-American bias, I hasten to

add that this was the tournament in which Britain's Peter Alliss had the mortifying experience of 5-putting from 15 ft on the 11th green.

A glance through the records will produce plenty more examples of leading pros. whose games have deserted them for reasons beyond their ken. Nicklaus, Brewer, Palmer, Casper and Player, for instance, all arrived at Carnoustie for the 1968 British Open without a single tournament win to their credit that season.

In the course of preparing this book I had some correspondence with the Professional Golfers' Association of America. In a letter, Bud Harvey, the Association's Director of Public Relations, wrote: ". . . it's difficult to get two professionals together in a discussion of teaching techniques without launching a debate". I'm sure he will forgive me for suggesting that what you start is not so much a debate as an argument.

This confusion and uncertainty is naturally reflected at the level of the ordinary club golfer. Some young players get down to scratch in a very short time. Others, often more athletic, practise and practise yet seem to stick at a handicap of around 15 for their entire playing lives. Some players who achieve scratch in their 'teens find themselves struggling to play off 6 at twenty-eight, have declined to a handicap of 12 by thirty-eight, and are abandoning the game altogether at forty-eight. Also, consistency is a rare quality, and it is quite common for a player off 15 to play to 6 one day and 24 the next.

I, myself, took up golf in 1947 at the age of thirty-four. I brought to the game a good deal of the kind of scientific knowledge (mathematics and physics) which is helpful in understanding "technical" sports. I had a lot of athletic experience behind me. I was in good physical shape and, in fact, trained the following year as a possible British representative in the pole vault event at the 1948 Olympics.

Yet I found golf extremely difficult. It quickly became clear to me that teachers of the game did not have a firm grasp of what they were trying to do or teach. One said: "Do this." Another said: "Do that." One book said: "This is the correct method." Another said: "That is the correct method." I used to ask. "Why?" Only rarely did I receive a sound reason for what I had been told to do. Then—as, indeed, now—the whole approach to the game was so illogical and unmethodical that golf could be regarded as an art rather than what it should be, a science.

Nevertheless, I managed by assiduous practice to get my handicap down to 9 in the first year and 6 in the second. Within a few years I was playing off 2. I was not happy with my game, however. Some days I played extremely well but there were others—and every golfer will know what I mean—when I scuffed and fluffed my way around the course and nothing seemed to go right. Even when I actually played to my handicap, I was aware that I struck the ball very indifferently.

I knew that my technique was at fault. I therefore set out to try to find a new one rather than to try to reduce my handicap further with the muddled means at my disposal. For inspiration I turned to other technical sports, such as the shot putt, discus, javelin and pole vault, in which the improvements in standards during this century have been dramatic.

HIT WITH THE LEGS

A glance at the Olympic figures is sufficient to establish the spectacular progress made in field athletics during this century. These are the winning performances down the years:

SHOT PUTT

1900	46 ft	3 in
1924	49 ft	2¼ in
1936	53 ft	1¾ in
1952	57 ft	1½ in
1968	67 ft	4¾ in

JAVELIN

1908	179 ft	10½ in
1924	206 ft	6½ in
1936	235 ft	8½ in
1952	242 ft	0½ in
1968	295 ft	7¼ in

DISCUS

1900	118 ft	3 in
1924	151 ft	5 in
1936	165 ft	7½ in
1952	180 ft	6½ in
1968	212 ft	6½ in

POLE VAULT

1900	10 ft	10 in
1924	12 ft	11½ in
1936	14 ft	3¼ in
1952	14 ft	11¼ in
1968	17 ft	8½ in

Development of the fibreglass pole has, of course, played a significant part in pole vaulting since the last war, but it has only exaggerated the existing trend. Otherwise it is clear that the "natural" athletes of the early part of this century, Olympic record holders in their time, would hardly be of club standard in competition with the "technical" athletes of today.

In all the above sports there has been an evolution of method over the years. It has in each case taken place in stages and followed a very clear course.

Stage 1. Initially the arms and hands were used to provide the power with a braced body to push from (shot putt, 1900–24, 46 ft 3 inches–49 ft 2¼ inches).

Stage 2. The shoulders were used to generate power, whipping the arms and hands, and the legs and hips were braced to take the reaction (1936, 53 ft 1¾ inches).

Stage 3. The power came from the hip muscles which threw the top half of the body, the legs being braced to take the strain (1952, 57 ft 1½ inches).

Stage 4. A position of the body was discovered in which it became instinctive to drive with the legs and the rest of the body was whipped like a spring to fling the missile (1968, 67 ft 4¾ inches).

The advantage of using the legs rather than the hands and arms as a source of power are self-evident when you consider their comparative strength: a man can walk for hours on end, yet even a trained athlete can stand on his hands for only a minute or two. However, to use the legs as a source of power as they are employed in field athletics today requires an understanding of reflex muscle technique.

It was instinctive for the earliest shot putters to make *conscious* use of the hands and arms as their source of power: this is what we do when we are employing tools and implements in everyday life. In contrast, today's shot putters relax all the minor muscles (hips, back, shoulders, arm) in the chain between their legs and their hand. These minor muscles are then stretched by the inertia of the shot and, in the throw, used in *reflex*—that is, with no conscious effort—as elastic is used in a catapult. This

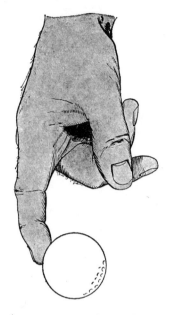

Fig. 1   Conscious Action

The ball is being moved by contracting the muscles of the finger. This is a conscious action, the finger muscles pulling against a braced hand. It can be seen that the speed at which the ball can be moved is limited as the power available from the muscles of the single finger muscle is relatively small.

is the *only* efficient and scientific way to use the body when the object is to propel something, and it is the development and application of reflex muscle technique which is responsible for the vast improvement in field sports standards during this century.

The difference between conscious and reflex use of muscles is simply illustrated in Figs. 1 and 2. In Fig. 1 the forefinger is moving the ball by contracting the muscles of the finger while bracing the hand. This is a conscious movement and it is the finger which is generating the power. In Fig. 2 the power

23

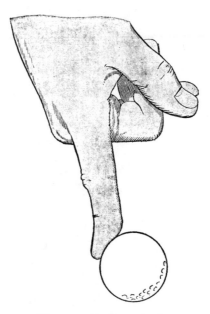

Fig. 2   Reflex Action

The ball is being moved by power transmitted through the finger from the arm. As the relaxed finger meets the ball, it flexes, and, as the ball moves, the reflex action of the finger applies far more power and speed to the ball than is possible with a conscious action by the finger. The source of power is actually the arm—the finger merely absorbs the power as it is flexed and then, by a reflex action, transmits it to the ball—and a braced body provides a reaction to the arm movement.

comes from the arm and the relaxed finger is bent back as contact is made with the ball, energy is stored up in the stretched muscle of the finger and this energy is released as the ball is moved.

The perfect technique which has now been evolved for field athletics is a sophisticated technique requiring a series of *exact* positions of the body so that the power can be transmitted directly from the

24

legs to the hand. If these positions are not achieved, a conscious movement has to be made with one or more of the minor muscles whereupon the legs can no longer be employed as the direct source of power and the reflex chain breaks down.

Earlier I used the expressions "natural" and "technical" athletes. This is not to suggest that there is anything *un*-natural in the way body muscles are used in modern field athletics techniques. The point is that the required positions are not positions an athlete would drop into instinctively. He requires expert tuition and must then, by repeating them thousands of times, muscle-memorise movements which are basically foreign to his nature until eventually they become as instinctive and natural as the movements he makes when using a knife and fork. Adoption of technical methods also requires a fundamental change in outlook on the part of an athlete who finds that his performances worsen until such time as he has mastered the technique.

The photographs (Figs. 3a–3d) of an athlete throwing a javelin is one of the best examples of a position from which leg thrust can be transmitted through relaxed and flexed muscles to give maximum power and speed through the hand. The most interesting aspect is the position of the right arm when fully extended. It has been turned clockwise so that the muscles and tendons of the shoulder, elbow and wrist are fully flexed and thus able to transmit the power of the legs to the hand. This position may look unnatural at first glance but it is, in fact, merely an illustration of the surprising way muscles can be stretched if they are relaxed.

In my own athletics career I had an interesting demonstration of how difficult it is to improve at technical sports if you approach them on the wrong

25

a

b

c

d

Figs 3a-d

26

Figs. 3a–3d

By a run-up and crossover step this javelin
thrower has put himself in a position where the
inertia of his run and the drive of his legs is
transmitted to his hand. From the golf point of
view it is the position of the right arm which is
of interest. It has been turned clockwise to give
a position of the elbow, wrist and shoulder in
which the power of the legs can be transmitted
to the hand through a flexed body. In this
position it is instinctive to drive with the legs.

Photo: Toni Nett

lines. I had decided, after winning the New Zealand championship within nine months of taking up pole vaulting, that this was the sport for me, and, after arriving in England late in 1936, I practised with dedication nearly every day for more than two years.

My performance did not improve by a single inch.

At that time the muscle technique I have outlined above was not understood in Britain. In the summer of 1939, however, I went on an A.A.A. course at Loughborough College where they had the Harvard University field events coach as guest. He watched me and asked: "What are you trying to do?" I explained. "Yes," he said, "your aim is correct but you do not understand the basic athletic principle involved." He then went into the matter of storing power in the muscles by stretching them.

In the next three months my performance improved by a foot.

To return to golf, when I found myself dissatisfied with my own game, I set out to try to apply field athletic techniques, to find a way of transmitting the power of the legs directly to the hands. Now, after the better part of fifteen years of thought and trial, I have evolved a swing in which the legs are the power-house and all the other muscles of the body—shoulders, back, hips, arms wrist and hands—are used in reflex in a way which is both athletically and scientifically sound.

Two main problems faced me in my quest. Firstly, I had to find a right arm position equivalent to the position of the right arm of the modern javelin thrower. This was not too difficult and Fig. 4 shows a hitting position which satisfies the requirements. Secondly—and much more difficult—was finding an address position and executing a backswing which would bring me instinctively into this hitting position. That, basically, is what this book is all about.

It is probably worth saying what effect this method has had on my own game. At fifty-eight, I am hitting the ball farther, straighter and to a more consistent length with the varying clubs than at any time in my golfing life. Although I am 5 ft 8 inches tall and weigh only 11 stones, I am as long off the tee—around 280 yards in summer conditions—as low handicap players half my age and considerably bigger in size. I rarely find myself in the rough and, when I do, it is almost inevitably because I haven't been concentrating. I do, naturally, hit bad shots from time to time—who doesn't?—but I no longer experience those depressing rounds when nothing seems to go right. On one of the days when I'm really "off", I simply tend to push the ball off line.

Subjective experience, of course, is of limited value to others. I am quite certain, however, that the method I have developed is not merely right for me. I believe that with practice, preferably a little each day, it can help anyone to play better golf and, what's more, to go on improving in normal circumstances well into their 60s. I make this second claim because this method is based on well-founded scientific and athletic principles which give a golfer a logical pattern for the development of his swing over the years with a corresponding gradual improvement in his game.

It may, at first, seem a far-fetched notion to try to apply field event techniques to a game so vastly different as golf. I would point out, however, that they have also been applied in recent years to skiing, which has been revolutionised by shifting the emphasis from the upper part of the body to the legs.

I feel I should also answer the immediate objections

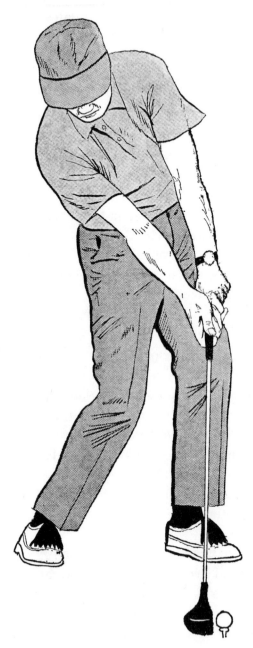

Fig. 4

Fig. 4   Ideal Impact Position

The position of the right arm is equivalent to the position of the right arm of the javelin thrower. The elbow is forward to the right hip and the arm has been put in a position where it can be used in reflex. The right elbow is several inches forward of the position of any golfer to date. How to achieve this hitting position is the theme of this book.

that will be raised to the effect that the average pro. today already gets his legs into the shot. This is true, but only in the sense that they brace them or co-ordinate them with the hips, hands and arms. They do not *generate* the swing with the legs, deriving power from the legs alone and using all their other muscles in reflex.

I hope to show the "why" as well as the "how" and I like to think this book will prove a manual to which anyone having trouble with their game can return and, with a little thought, iron out their problems.

I have, incidentally, chosen the title *The Golf Swing Of The Future* for this book not merely because I believe it contains the only golf technique which is both athletically and scientifically sound. If you look at the golf swing historically, this technique also pushes to a logical conclusion the evolutionary process which been taking place over the years.

PAST AND PRESENT

One of the factors which makes golf such a difficult game is that you are using a club with an off-centre head. The result is that any acceleration of the club produces a rotating force on the hands which the hand muscles try to resist. This effect explains the form taken by the early golf swing.

As with the early shot putters, it was instinctive for the early golfers to use their arms to generate power, and to whip their hands and hit against a braced body. It felt good—natural, if you like—to roll the clubface open on the backswing, back to square on the downswing, then shut after impact. By swinging the club in this way, the grip felt comfortable and easy.

The fundamental differences between that early swing and the modern golf swing are that, in the accepted method today, the hips have become the source of power and rolling of the wrists has been greatly reduced. Golf, in fact, may be said to be hovering today around the halfway stage in the process of evolution which field athletics have gone through.

At this point it is worth analysing the swings of yesterday and today in some detail to emphasise the aspects in which they differ and to get the way the swing has developed into some kind of perspective.

The method I have adopted is to break the old Scottish swing and the modern swing down into five parts—the address, the takeaway, the top of the swing, the first movement down and the hitting area—and to dissect each in turn.

33

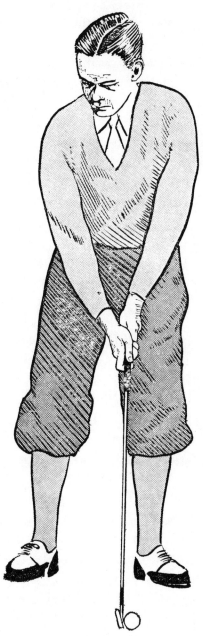

Fig. 5

Fig. 5   The Address Position Yesterday

This was a relaxed position with the hands just forward of centre. Both toes were slightly turned out. The ball was taken off the left heel for the driver and about an inch farther back for the 3-wood and 4-wood. As the irons became more lofted the ball was positioned farther back until the wedge was taken off the right foot. The stance varied with each club. For the driver it was shut and then opened progressively through the range of clubs. For the wedge the stance could be as much as 45 degrees open. The left hand adopted a three- or four-knuckle grip. The knees were almost straight.

Fig. 6

Fig. 6   The Address Position Today

**This is a more positive position. The left arm
and the club are in line and the hands are well
forward of centre. The right foot is square and
the left foot is turned 25 degrees or more
towards the target. The left hand has a two-
knuckle grip with the left thumb on top of the
shaft. The ball is taken off the left heel for all
shots. The stance is usually square but it is
sometimes slightly shut for the driver and
slightly open for the short irons. The knees are
bent and the back is straight.**

Fig. 7   The Takeaway Yesterday

The swing has been started from a press with the hands. The club is taken back inside and the clubface is opened. The body pivots about the right leg. The weight is being transferred to the right foot.

Fig. 8   The Takeaway Today

The swing has been started by a press of the right knee. The club has been taken straight back from the ball, slightly hooded. The takeaway is in one piece. There is little hip turn and the shoulders are turning on the hips. The knees are bent.

39

Fig. 9

Fig. 9   The Top of the Swing Yesterday

The body has pivoted around the right leg. The hips have turned almost as much as the shoulders. The wrists have cocked and the clubface is open. The left wrist is concave and the club points at the target. The weight has been transferred to the right foot and the left heel has come up off the ground. It is a well-balanced position.

Fig. 10

Fig. 10   The Top of the Swing Today

The shoulders have turned 90 degrees and the hip turn has been restricted to 45 degrees. The left wrist is flat. The clubface is square. There has been a limited weight shift to the inside of the right foot. The left heel has rolled towards the right foot. This is a very compact position for a controlled short-iron shot. However, for a wooden club the hands would be higher and the hips would turn a little more.

Fig. 11   The First Movement Down Yesterday

The weight has moved to the left foot and the left heel is firmly on the ground. The left side has started to brace. The hands have come straight to waist level and the clubface is open. The concave left wrist at the top has dictated this movement. The hit will be from inside to out.

44

Fig. 12   The First Movement Down Today

**The knees have moved towards the left and the
club and hands are coming down steeply on to
the ball. This is possible only if the left wrist is
flat at the top of the swing.**

45

Figs. 13 and 14   The Hitting Area Yesterday

The weight has been transferred to the left and the left side is braced. The hit is with the arms, the right arm rolling over the left. The essence of the swing is to move into a firm, braced and

46

Fig. 14

relatively still position of the body so that the arms can be used to bring the rolling clubface into contact at exactly the right instant. The power is obtained more by clubhead speed than by the pressure at contact.

Fig. 15

Fig. 16

Figs. 15 and 16   The Hitting Area Today

The right elbow is hugging the right side as the body, arms and club move in one piece through the ball. The rolling of the right arm over the left is co-ordinated with the leg and hip movement. Only the top players get a reflex action of the hands. The clubface is rolling through but to a much lesser extent than in the old method. The whole pressure of the body is behind the shot and this gives better flighting and more accurate control of length. Bad shots are less destructive. The hit is only slightly from inside to out.

49

The early, natural swing produced great, natural golfers who dominated the game. The modern, more technical, swing has resulted in a marked and general improvement in playing standards. There are two basic reasons for this. The first is the shift in the source of power from the hands and arms to the far stronger, and therefore far more reliable, hips. The second is the reduction in wrist-rolling and the fact that what rolling there is takes place over a much larger arc in the modern swing and is consequently easier to control.

The benefits of the modern swing compared with the old may be summarised as follows:

1. Shots are consistently straighter and even mishits are not so destructive. In other words, with the old-fashioned swing, a shot pulled to the left was likely to be hooked as well. Similarly, if you pushed the ball to the right, the error would probably be exaggerated by a slice as well.

2. The quick hook is rare.

3. More pressure can be applied to the ball at impact, which means that it is better flighted (i.e. has a more correct relationship between forward speed and backspin), travels farther and "dies" quickly on landing, an important element in accuracy of length.

4. Mistiming causes less damage. If, for example, you are chipping with the hands and arms and hit the ground behind the ball, you will fluff whereas with the far stronger hips, back and shoulders being used to drag the clubhead through the ball, you will still get away with a reasonable shot.

5. This knowledge gives confidence. Thus the modern game stands up better under pressure. In

moments of stress it is the arms and hands, particularly the hands, which tend to crack under the demands of executing a precision shot in which timing is all-important. Even at critical points in a modern tournament, with perhaps thousands of pounds or dollars hanging on a vital chip to the last green, you seldom see the fluffs which were common in the old days.

With all this said, the modern swing—by which I mean the square-to-square swing—is, from a scientific and athletic point of view, far from perfect. The clubface is still turning over at impact (although not as much as in the old-fashioned swing), and it is only at impact that the clubface is square to the direction in which it is travelling. Thus, if the ball is struck just before the clubface is square, there will be a slight fade. Correspondingly, if it is struck just after it is square, there will be a slight draw. Some professionals adapt their swing to produce a slight draw or a slight fade as they feel they can control the ball better if they know which way it will move. Thus they settle for hitting the ball just before the clubface is square or just after. This is not really a scientific way of bringing the club into contact with the ball and, not surprisingly, even the most distinguished pros. hit very indifferent shots from time to time.

Again, from an athletic point of view, the modern swing can never be made a completely natural and instinctive action no matter how often the movements are repeated in practice. This is because the whole accent, including the defensive measure of a weak left hand position, is on eliminating the hook by preventing the strong right side from dominating the swing. Thus, instead of using the strong right side instinctively, the golfer has to remind himself constantly to make the conscious effort to pull with the left side to generate the swing.

While it is true that the square-to-square method has produced to date far more competent golfers than any previous concept, the modern golfer is always extremely conscious of his swing and produces it mechanically, almost to numbers. The result is the inhibition of natural flair. Furthermore, in the modern swing the right elbow is hugged to the side through the hitting area so that the club, arms and body move in one piece through the ball, the right arm is tight and the hand action tends to be a conscious hit rather than a reflex action. Wherever you have conscious action, you suffer loss of feel on which, in turn, accuracy of length depends.

I think it is significant that the square-to-square method, although good, is not in itself so superior that all the "greats" are obliged to adopt it. Player has dismissed it publicly: Casper and Trevino, two more of the finest players of our time, certainly do not use the square-to-square method. They are great natural players and have developed their own individual way of golf. Both Casper and Trevino, for example, employ the strong, not the weak, grip with the left hand and have the left thumb behind the shot.

It is therefore logical to assume that there must be a better method than the present one and that there is a long way to go before we can say that the ultimate in technique has been reached and been accepted universally as the last word in method.

IT'S PRESSURE THAT COUNTS

It is widely accepted that the critical factor in determining the distance a golf ball travels is clubhead speed at impact. This is not true. Supporters of that view do their mathematics on the assumption that the clubhead is a freely-moving object colliding with a golf ball. In fact, a golf club is not a freely-moving object. It is an extension of the body, gripped by the hands, and the critical factor in determining the distance a golf ball travels is *pressure* applied to it or, to put this in a more scientific way, the application of force through a distance.

All golfers, even those who will still argue that clubhead speed at impact is all that matters, have had personal experiences on the golf course which indicate the truth of what I have said. Take, for example, the man who normally dislocates his swing by the violence he uses trying to generate clubhead speed and who, finding himself faced with a lateral ditch, decides to play short. He swings at a fraction of his normal speed, he stays behind the ball and— plop!—he's in the ditch because he has hit a firm, slow golf shot and the ball has travelled 30 yards farther than he anticipated.

After he won the British Open at windy Lytham St. Annes, Tony Jacklin was reported as saying: "I had to keep reminding myself that the slower I swung, the farther the ball would go." He was, in effect, making the point that it's pressure that counts.

The technique set out later in this book, using the muscles of the body efficiently, gives power without

53

effort. However, as the muscles are being stretched and used in reflex, time is needed for this process to take place. Therefore the club *must* be swung slowly. But, in demonstrating this technique, one of the most common psychological barriers I encounter is in getting people to accept that it is not necessary to make a quick and violent assault on the ball. Yet no one has difficulty in accepting that, if you are hammering a nail into a piece of wood, it is not the speed of the hammerhead that gets results but the pressure you apply at the moment of impact and immediately after.

It is the same in all sports where a ball has to be hit. The bat or racquet has to be swung as an extension of the body through a grip which firms up at impact, enabling the wrists to act in reflex and so transmit the power of the body to the bat or racquet. Tennis is a good example. Even with a highly-strung racquet the ball goes nowhere at all if the grip is slack. If it is firm, however, you generate tremendous power and have the feeling that the ball is in contact with the racquet for an appreciable time.

In the light of this it is worth considering what happens when you hit a golf ball. In the perfect shot the acceleration from the top is constant and the shaft of the club is bowed slightly as the head is dragged down. At impact, as the pressure is being kept up with the hands, the bowing of the shaft is increased as the ball is compressed against the face of the club. Then the shaft rebounds, still with the ball on the face, and, as it straightens, the compressed ball pushes itself off from the clubface, having first picked up the speed of the clubhead. The ball can take off at almost twice the speed of the clubhead.

The amount the shaft bends and rebounds at impact, and the length of time the ball is in contact

54

with the clubface, picking up bonus power, is in direct proportion to the amount of pressure behind the shot. To put this another way, it has been demonstrated that the force of impact with the ball can reduce the speed of the clubhead from 100 m.p.h. to 80 m.p.h. It follows that, if you can keep the pressure up through the ball, you can have the clubhead travelling at 85 m.p.h. or, if you are strong enough, even 90 m.p.h. This keeps the clubhead in contact with the ball for a longer time and dictates the distance the ball will travel.

If your grip gives at impact, the ball may be on the face of the club for only $\frac{1}{2}$ an inch. A grip which firms up at impact, transmitting the body power and making full use of the elasticity of the shaft of the club, can increase the distance to $\frac{3}{4}$ of an inch, and, because the ball is on the club that $\frac{1}{4}$ inch longer, it goes considerably farther for the same clubhead speed. This increased contact between club and ball also gives you far greater control over the shot.

If you watch players like Arnold Palmer and Jack Nicklaus pitching, you would think from the speed at which they swing the iron that they were playing a shot of about 30 yards. Yet you find the ball landing on the green 70 or 80 yards away.

Pressure—the application of a force through a distance—is not merely important in terms of how far the ball will travel. It also governs the manner in which the distance of the shot is obtained. Pressure ensures that the ball is well-flighted—that is, it has the correct amount of backspin to keep it in the air while the momentum of the shot is carrying it forward.

You will notice that women rarely flight the ball well. This is because their hands are not strong enough to keep the pressure up through the ball.

With the majority of women, therefore, a golf shot is a "collision" between the clubhead and the ball instead of the application of force through a distance. The result is that they achieve most of their length by the ball rolling along the ground.

The only way to achieve accuracy in golf is to swing the club at a speed which enables you to have it under complete control at all times, apply the correct pressure to the ball and thus flight it properly so that distance is obtained in the air. The ball which leaves the tee like a bullet is badly flighted and is either disappointingly short or gets its length by bounding along the fairway, and, all too frequently, bounding into the rough. The well-flighted shot starts slowly, climbs steadily, keeps going and "dies" quickly on landing. On a short hole, if your opponent says: "Well hit, but you're going to be short," yet the ball lands safely on the green, you can normally be sure that you have struck a well-flighted shot.

Golf clubs are designed as precision instruments but they can be used with precision only if the ball is well-flighted. I remember once watching Ben Hogan practising for the Canada Cup. Starting with the wedge, he worked his way down through the irons, then through the woods. With each change of club his caddy moved back 10 yards and caught the ball first bounce, even the drives. This was possible solely because Ben Hogan flights the ball so well. I am not, of course, suggesting that the ordinary club golfer, who lacks the time to hit several hundred golf balls every day the year around, can hope to achieve this standard of accuracy. Nevertheless it is the model he should have before him.

It is always a good idea to decide exactly what you are trying to do before you try to do it, and, before moving on to the details of what I believe will be the swing of the future, I think it is worth having a look at the various departments of the game.

The Tee Shot. Is the object to hit the ball farther than everyone else? Of course not. Naturally, every golfer derives tremendous satisfaction from out-driving the other three players in a four-ball, but anyone whose reputation rests simply on long hitting is seldom a good competitor. The object should be a reasonable and consistent length, plus accuracy of direction, plus the confidence that you have the power and ability to hit the ball that bit harder when necessary. The reason for this is that most modern courses, and the good ones in particular, are designed for a positioned tee shot on the long holes, both from the point of view of making the second shot easier and from the fact that fairways tend to narrow around 220 or 230 yards and threaten trouble to the shot that is only slightly off line and does not "die" quickly. Even on the hardest and driest fairway, the well-flighted shot will not run un-duly far after landing. If I may return to Ben Hogan, in a tournament you would find his tee shots on the long holes ending up in much the same spot in each of the four rounds. This is what everyone should aim at. It has the additional advantage that you can establish how short or how long the course is play-ing by using your tee shot as a measure.

The Fairway Wood. This, too, should be a precision shot. It is important to be straight, but it is even more important to hit it an accurate length. You have to be extremely inaccurate in direction to be 20 yards to the left or right, but if your length tends to vary widely you are uncertain which club to take and how to hit. Consequently you can be 30 or 40

57

yards too long or too short. Here it is even more important than with the drive to get distance in the air if you are to get accuracy in length. For example, you are faced with a distant bunker, then 50 yards of fairway to the green. If your wood shots normally run 45 yards after landing, you must pitch the ball just over the bunker. Otherwise, assuming the shot to be straight, you will probably go right through the green. On the other hand, if you know the ball will "die" within 10 yards of its point of impact, you have 40 yards to play with. Thus on most good courses there is no problem if you can hit an accurate length that is all carry.

The Irons. These can be considered under one heading. With the irons you are getting within striking distance of the pin and should be aiming for a single putt. One way of registering progress is by the number of putts you hole off irons to the green. It is obvious that you have to be reasonably straight, but the important aspect of iron play is again accuracy in length. If you do not have it in your command you are immediately confused over which club to take. It is this striving for accuracy in length with the irons that has been mainly responsible for the changes in golfing technique which have taken place over the years.

The irons are designed to give a variation of distance of approximately 10 to 15 yards between each club. to achieve this result it is vital to hit the ball correctly. The inclination, particularly with the shorter irons, is to hit the ball flat on the face of the club, which means that you can get several yards more distance with the shot than either you or the clubmaker envisaged. When the club is placed on the ground you should imagine a plane at right-

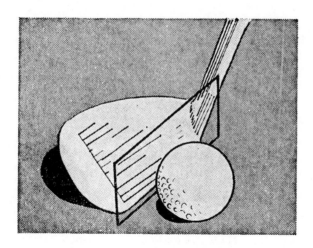

Fig. 17   The Hitting Plane

**Each club is designed to hit the ball a set length
according to the golfer using it. The difference,
for example, between a No. 3 and No. 4 iron, or
between a No. 5 and No. 6 iron, is 10 yards for
medium hitters and 15 yards for long hitters.
This accuracy in length is possible only if you
visualise hitting the ball with the illustrated
plane and not with the flat of the clubface.**

angles to the ground from the front edge of the club.
It is this plane which you should feel hit the ball
(Fig. 17). It was difficult to do this consistently with
the early golf swing in which there was pronounced
rolling of the wrists and timing was consequently
critical, and even today, when wrist roll has been
reduced and takes place over a much longer period,
it is still by no means easy.

Striking the ball correctly, which in turn ensures
that it is properly flighted, is even more important
with the irons—a scoring shot—than with the woods.
The player who has to play short of an open green
because he knows the ball will run is always

at the mercy of a bad bounce and can never go for the pin with any confidence, while, if faced with the task of negotiating a bunker flanking the green, he must either play deliberately short or risk going right through the green and into whatever trouble lies behind it. The aim should be to know precisely which club you need and to be reasonably certain that if you pitch the ball on the green it will stay there.

The Chip. If you feel you can get down in two from around the green providing you concentrate, you can win almost any match. Chipping straight is not all that difficult. It is accuracy of length that is important because, with the chip, you should be going for the hole, not merely for the green.

The Putt. Here again direction is a fairly simple matter and it is accuracy of length which is the vital factor. If you master this, it is surprising how often you can hole the long one, even under pressure (and golf under pressure is an entirely different game from golf).

You may say that the standards I have outlined in this look at the various departments of the game are impossible for the part-time golfer. I do not agree. Accuracy of length, the most important aspect of all golf shots, is simply a matter of good technique and practice—there is, it must be said, no short cut to good golf—and I am confident that the principles outlined in this book can put it within the grasp of the average golfer.

Many players say that they have no desire to achieve a high standard but merely wish to enjoy themselves. This, I feel, is self-delusion. There can be small satisfaction in playing a game badly and, if you do not take golf seriously, you might as well get your exercise by taking the dog for a walk. Besides, the handicapping system becomes a farce if a golfer never knows what kind of performance he is going to put up. The day you play to 6 off a handicap of 15, you are cheating, and the day you play to 24 you are wasting your opponent's time.

To be philosophical about the subject, one of the greatest sources of pleasure in life is physical prowess. To make your body submit to your will and acquire some new skill is an expression of your individual personality and gives you a satisfied feeling that can be more enduring and rewarding than any other sensation from music to sex. You get out of the game only what you put into it, and, in my experience, the player who derives the most satisfaction out of golf is the one who is aspiring to single figures and sees some hope of getting there. I hope this book will help many golfers to achieve this target and, because the technique I have evolved ensures that you make the best use of the power available in the body, will enable older enthusiasts to postpone by many years the decision to take out non-playing membership and seek their pleasure at the card table, in the snooker room or at the 19th hole.

Developing a technique is a protracted task. Yet it is only by adopting and mastering a sound technique that steady progress can be made at the game. The ideal with all shots should be to hit the ball straight and to an accurate length. In order to do this the club has to be swung slowly and deliberately, and the ball has to be hit solidly with the full pressure of the body behind the shot. It's pressure that counts —and achieving maximum pressure should be the goal to which everything else is subordinated.

THE GOLF SWING OF THE FUTURE

From the start of my quest for an athletic and scientific swing I realised that progress could be made only by developing a swing in which the position of the right elbow at the hit was at least six inches farther forward—towards the centre of the body—than the present accepted position. This corresponds to the extended right-arm position of the modern javelin thrower and enables the power to be poured directly from the legs to the clubhead.

Over the years I have built in swings and modified them to achieve this aim. The recurrent problem I encountered was the question of opening and closing the clubface during the swing. The reason why the club opens on the backswing—even in the so-called square-to-square method it opens 90 degrees—is that, when the club is held in two hands with a conventional grip, the wrists would have to dislocate if the face was to remain square to the direction of travel as with, say, a tennis racquet.

This opening and closing of the clubface means that you are trying to hit the ball with the face of a club which is rotating in two planes. Golf must therefore be a difficult game. This difficulty is illustrated graphically in Figs. 18 and 19. The position of the hammer in Fig. 18 corresponds to the way a golf club was used in the past. Fig. 19 corresponds to the way it is used today. The complications which arise from using a hammer—or a golf club—in this way are self-evident.

An even more vital point is that you cannot develop a swing in which the legs are the source of

63

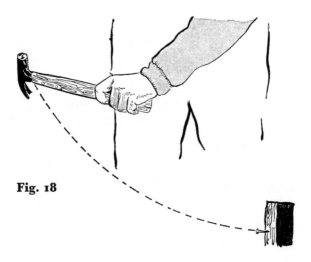

Fig. 18

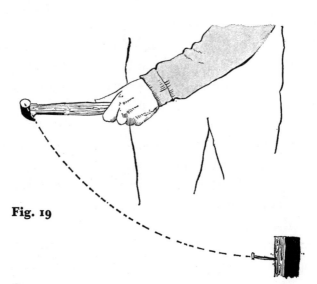

Fig. 19

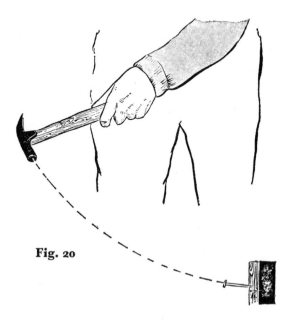

Fig. 20

Figs. 18, 19 and 20

These drawings of a hammer being used in a
similar stroke action to that involved in hitting
a golf ball with a club to show how complicated
a path the hitting surface of the club travels.
The reason is that a golf club has an off-centre
head, which produces a rotating force on the
hands when it is swung, and we have insisted
in hitting the ball with an inflexible, two-
handed grip. Fig. 18 corresponds with the old-
fashioned swing, Fig. 19 with the modern,
square-to-square method. Fig. 20 illustrates
the way a hammer would be used naturally.

power and the rest of the body is used in reflex if you have rolling of the wrists.

Fig. 20 shows the natural position which anyone using a hammer would adopt. There is no rolling of the wrist and the head of the hammer has remained square to the direction of travel. Could a golf club be used in the same way? My breakthrough came when I found a grip which enabled my left hand to swing the club like a hammer while the right hand moved relative to the left so that it locked in a powerful hitting grip, like a two-handed tennis backhand, at the top of the swing. I realise that quizzical eyebrows will be raised at the notion of a deliberate grip change during the swing. Yet, in any other two-handed action, whether it is baseball, cricket or chopping with an axe, there is always a change of grip on the backswing.

Before enlarging on this subject we should consider the foundation on which all else depends—posture.

POSTURE

You cannot play good golf without good posture. In posture I include the relative position of the hips and shoulders, the position of the feet, knees, head and arms, and the way you distribute your weight. They are the foundation of all types of swing and all the old standard "musts"—bracing the left side, getting behind the ball, hitting past the chin and so on—are closely bound up with them. Furthermore, it is impossible to develop a sound, repetitive swing if the posture at the address is bad or varies from shot to shot. On the other hand, once a good posture has been assumed, you can have a bad grip, or lift the club up with your arms, or even wave it around your

66

head, but you will still be able to hit the ball reasonably well.

Actually, I doubt whether more than five amateur golfers in a hundred, at any level of the game, have a sound posture. The contortions of most Sunday morning swings are the result of trying to compensate for a bad one, and so are the majority of quick hooks, wild slices and raised heads. Posture is the foundation of the swing and, if your golf goes off, nine times out of ten the cause will be bad posture.

Assuming a good hip–shoulder relationship at the address is by far the most difficult part of the swing. The ideal in the old swing was for the shoulders to turn through 90 degrees and the hips through 70 degrees. In the modern swing, while the shoulders still turn 90 degrees, and hips turn 45 degrees or less. With practically all bad golfers the hips turn as much as the shoulders. There is then no tension in the body because the back muscles have not been stretched, and the only way back to the ball is by pulling round with the shoulders. The outcome is loss of distance and a hook or slice of varying degrees of violence.

If you can stand in front of a mirror and try turning the shoulders to the right without turning the hips you will see how difficult it is, with or without a club, unless the starting position is correct. The hips will always collapse (that is, turn with the shoulders) if the shoulders are turned towards the target just a fraction more than the hips at the address, and the simple action of placing the right hand below the left on the club, or of taking a last look at the distant hole, can put you in this false position. It is basically a question of anatomy. The pelvis forms the junction between the spine and legs. The spine is attached to the pelvis semi-rigidly. On the other hand, the legs are attached to the pelvis by very flexible balljoints. It is this difference in flexibility which is at the root of the trouble. When we ask our muscles to turn our shoulders, the natural and easy way is to let the flexible hip joints turn. This inclination has to be inhibited by bracing the legs in such a way that the contracting body muscles have something to pull against and it becomes an instinctive and natural movement to turn the shoulders without turning the hips.

The ideal at the address is to have the hips slightly open relative to the shoulders. The shoulders will then turn more than the hips on the backswing, the shoulder and back muscles will be fully extended, and, at the top of the swing, there is a substantial increase in stored power for the shot.

Over the years I tried many methods of achieving an efficient hip–shoulder relationship. I found many that seemed to work. However, they were always more of a feeling than a position and, in trying to retain the feeling, I would exaggerate and lose it. I now consider I have found the solution. I turn the knees and feet towards the target, keeping the shoulders parallel to the line of flight. The left foot is turned about 30 degrees and the right foot 10 degrees or more. This gives the pelvis support to provide a firm base on which to rotate the spine. It is a position which is easily checked. Once the feet are in place it is relatively simple to line up the shoulders. This relative position of the hips and shoulders, produced by turning the feet and knees towards the target, works for any type of golf swing.

It is not a question of being supple. Once the right foot is turned 10 degrees towards the hole and the knees pressed to the left, a good hip–shoulder relationship can be assumed by practically every-

Fig. 21

**There are very few people who cannot turn
their shoulders 90 degrees without turning the
hips providing the hips are anchored. There is
therefore no reason to complicate the backswing by letting the hips turn. It detracts from
the power of the shot and makes it more
difficult to maintain balance.**

body, and it is easy, even for the stiffest person, to
make an adequate turn with the shoulders accompanied by a relatively small amount of give in the
hips. In Fig. 21 the person in the chair has no difficulty in making a 90-degree shoulder turn with his
hips anchored.

The address position I have suggested is an athletic
position. At the top of the backswing it produces a

position in which it is instinctive to start the down-swing with the legs and there is no inclination to pull round with the shoulders. It is not necessary to worry about bad backs. Bad backs are far more likely to be caused by trying to hit with a faulty posture in which your joints are at a mechanical disadvantage. A weak back will be strengthened, and a bad one possibly improved, by using it in conjunction with a good posture, exercising it as it should be exercised.

Other aspects of posture are detailed in the captions to the subsequent illustrations but I think it is worth summarising them here to complete this section.

The knees must be flexed and pushed towards the target just slightly.

The weight must be on the heels.

The head and shoulders must be absolutely square to the direction of the shot and behind the club. If you are not behind the club and the ball at the address, you will not be behind them at the moment of impact because, having pushed the club back on the backswing, you cannot get to the ball again without leading with the head and shoulders. The position of *the head* should be such that, after the stroke, the eyes come up in a vertical, not horizontal, plane with the right eye turning under the left eye. If the eyes turn in a horizontal plane, it means you have swung round with the shoulders.

The right arm, to be used in reflex, must be placed across the body at the address so that it is inside a vertical line through the balljoint of right hip. This elbow position hardly moves, relative to the shoulders, throughout the swing. The arm is turned so that the inside of the elbow joint faces away from the body.

The left arm hangs as near vertically as possible.

The grip I am advocating is unorthodox. It is really

the final touch to the swing and cannot be used effectively until the rest of the swing has been mastered
and built-in—i.e. the minimum of hip turn on the
backswing with a full shoulder turn, and a left arm
position at the top of the swing corresponding to that
shown in Fig. 39. This means you should be playing
well into single figures before attempting to adopt this
radical change.

The grip is exact with the hands almost at right
angles. With the *left hand* there is a strong, four-
knuckle grip. The shaft passes just under the upper
pad. The thumb, which should be approximately 45
degrees to the right of the centre of the shaft, is
pushed down, then pulled back, so that it feels very
firm. The *right hand*—of which the palm has been
turned outwards by the action of placing the right
arm across the body—is put on by taking the club in
the middle and third fingers and "screwing" the hand
to the left. The feel is that the club is held in the
finger tips of the right hand. Instead of the left
thumb fitting into the hollow of the right palm as in
an orthodox overlapping grip, the pad of the right
hand just touches the V formed by the left thumb
and forefinger. This grip enables the elbows to come
together naturally. It is important to feel tension in
the third, middle and index fingers of the right hand
when it is "screwed" on. This tension ensures that,
after a forward press, the clubface will automatically
turn under with the left thumb slipping into the hollow of the right hand to form what is known as the
strong, hooker's grip—a natural grip which puts
both hands in the right position to be used in reflex.
The sensation of a firm grip is provided by the left
thumb and its position throughout the swing is all-
important. You should always have it behind the
shaft, feeling pressure on it.

71

With the left arm vertical, the hands are very much nearer the body at the address than they are at the moment of impact. Therefore, at the address, the clubface should be placed not behind the ball but *inside* it. For chips, wedges and nine-irons the ball should be just off the toe of the club, one inch inside for other irons, and roughly two inches for woods. It is easier to make this adjustment than to have to contort the body and pull away from the ball in order to give the club room to go through.

The Forward Press

If the posture is correct, practically all faults in the golf swing stem from the method of starting it. It is essential to understand what a swing is. A great deal has been written about swinging the club as distinct from lifting it up and hitting with it. It has been said that it is like swinging a weight on the end of a string. This is not so. With a weight on the end of a string you have to move the centre of rotation to increase the centripetal force. A mental picture of a man whirling a lasso will clarify what I mean. In the golf swing we are concerned with the opposite of centripetal force—centrifugal force, or force tending to go away from you. The essential part of the swing is the building up of the centrifugal force of the club and body by using your muscles to accelerate the speed of rotation about a *fixed* point. The power is built up so that it can all be applied at the instant of impact.

The swing must always be started with a forward press. The reason is that the point of rotation is the neck and *this point must stay still throughout the swing.* It is not possible to keep it still repeatedly if you start the swing by a conscious effort from a stationary position. Such a conscious effort with one part of the body tends to move other parts of the body: it involves the contraction of muscles which exert a force on whatever part of the body they are pulling against. In the golf swing they are pulling against the neck, which you are trying to keep in a fixed position. The forward press, however, is the tensing of muscles in a stationary position so that the swing starts, without any tendency to move the neck, as soon as the muscles are relaxed.

With the swing described in this book, in which the power comes from the legs, the forward press should be made with both knees. If you press with the hands, you will find that you hit with the hands. If you press with one knee, you will hit with the hips. The forward press with both knees should be sufficient to press the clubhead, which is in contact with the ground, in the direction of the intended flight of the ball, thus bending the shaft of the club very slightly and increasing the tension on the hands, arms and body. Then, when you relax the body above the hips just a fraction, the whole swing starts.

Before moving on to the illustrations, it may be helpful to summarise some of the characteristics of the swing I am describing:

> With the clubface kept square to the direction of travel, a shot which is pushed will hook back on to the fairway and a shot which is pulled will slice back on to the fairway (the opposite of the result produced by the old Scottish swing).
> There is scarcely any weight transference.
> Rolling of the wrists is eliminated. Consequently, timing is virtually automatic, the position of the

ball in relation to the left foot is the same with all the clubs, and the feet are always placed so that a line through the heels is parallel with the line of the shot (although the stance narrows slightly, as today, as one comes down from the driver to the wedge).

It enables full use to be made of that instinctive and natural source of power, the right side, instead of trying to inhibit it as does the modern, square-to-square method.

Figs. 22, 23, 24   The Grip

The left hand has a strong, four-knuckle grip with the left thumb down the back of the shaft. The right hand is placed on the club by taking the shaft in the middle and third fingers and "screwing" the hand to the left. The feeling then is that the club is being held by the tips of the third, middle and index fingers of the right hand and that these fingers are under tension. The pad of the right hand just touches the V formed by the left thumb and forefinger. The arms are pressed together. This grip is my solution to the twin problems of being able to swing the club straight back with the clubface remaining square to the direction of travel and, at the same time, getting the right elbow into a position in which the power of the legs can be transmitted directly to the club. The left hand will take the club back and, as it is turned under, the left thumb will slip into the palm of the right hand, forming a very strong grip. This unorthodox grip, however, is advocated only for those who have already mastered the rest of the swing—i.e. a top-of-the-swing position which has the minimum

74

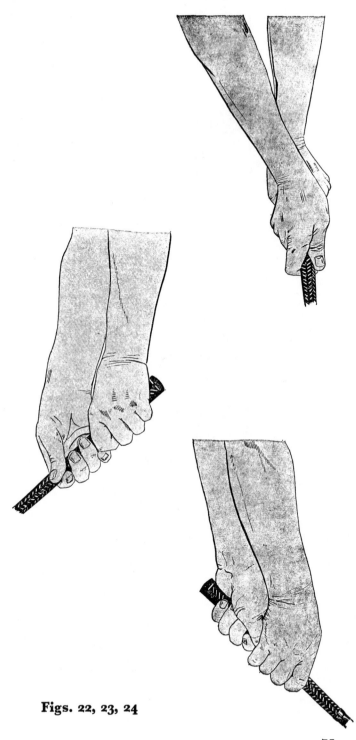

Figs. 22, 23, 24

75

Fig. 25

of hip turn with a full shoulder turn and a left arm position corresponding to that shown in Fig. 39. You should be playing well into single figures before attempting it.

Fig. 25   *The Address Position*

The shoulders are parallel to the intended line of flight. The left foot is turned 30 degrees to the left and the right foot 10 degrees or more to the left in order to restrict the hip turn on the backswing. The aim is to have a 90-degree shoulder turn and no hip turn so that the muscles of the shoulders and back are stretched as much as possible, providing greater power for the shot. The weight is equally distributed between the feet and is on the heels to ensure that you remain well-balanced as the club is swung back and your centre of gravity moves forward. The left arm is as near vertical as possible to enable you to swing it straight back (if the arms are away from the body you are forced to swing them around the body on the backswing). The right arm is across the body, inside the joint of the right hip (the right elbow stays virtually in the same position, relative to the shoulders, throughout the swing), and the inside of the elbow joint faces away from the body. The heels, like the shoulders, are parallel to the intended line of flight. The clubhead is placed inside the ball (two inches for woods, one inch for irons, just inside for chips) because, while there is an angle between the left arm and the club at the address, at the hit the arm and the club are to all intents and purposes in a straight line. With all clubs the ball is played off the left heel.

77

Figs. 26a and 26b   The Backswing

The swing is started with a forward press of the legs. Both knees are pushed towards the target slightly (about an inch), taking care the head is kept back. This position of the legs and hips is held and the takeaway is with the top part of the body alone. The rhythm is for the knees to move forward on the press, hold their position on the backswing and move forward again from the top. This is in contrast to the press with the right knee or hip, accompanied by slight

b

transference of weight and the hips turning 30–45
degrees on the backswing, which is favoured by
modern methods. I am trying to stop any transference
of weight and to get a counter-movement—that is,
the slight forward movement of the legs to counter
the backswing. With the clubhead resting on the
ground, the press forward with the legs increases the

tension on the hands. As this tension relaxes with completion of the forward press, the club is swung back very slowly, the left hand turned under the right in a reflex action from the press. The feeling is that the left arm is going under the right arm, that they are turning in the opposite direction from that in the old-type swing. In modern terms it would be said that the clubface is being shut although, in fact, it is merely being kept square to the direction of travel. At the halfway stage the left thumb has slipped into the palm of the right hand. The inertia of the swinging club is producing an anti-clockwise turning force on the right hand which is tensing the right elbow, forcing the elbows together. The club has been taken straight back from the ball in a steep arc. The hips feel as if they have not moved. The feet are firmly on the ground.

Fig. 27 *The Top of the Swing*

There has been a full shoulder turn. The right leg has remained as at the takeaway. The left hip has moved slightly to accommodate the shoulder turn, but it feels as if there has been no hip movement at all. Both feet are firmly on the ground. The clubface is in what, in modern parlance, would be called a tightly shut position. The left wrist is flat, or convex. The left thumb is still behind the shaft and the pressure of the club on the right fingers is keeping the right elbow under tension and pressed towards the left arm. The left arm has gone round the body hardly at all and feels as if it is in line with the target. The back and shoulder muscles have been fully stretched and the arms and hands are an extension of this tension. It is a position

Fig. 27

from which it is instinctive to drive with the legs. The position of the right elbow is all-important. If it were slightly farther round the body, the pressure on the right hand would not force the right elbow forward and the firm and flexed connection between the hands and body would be lost. In effect, it has been necessary to introduce a radical change in grip and stance, as well as in the takeaway, to get the right elbow in a position at the top of the swing which enables the right arm to be used in reflex like that of the javelin thrower.

Fig. 28   The First Movement Down

It is instinctive for the legs to start the down-swing. Both knees move towards the target. The pressure is felt on the left thumb and the left hand feels as if it is being twisted anti-clockwise. As the pressure increases and the right hand is bent backwards, the right elbow will come well forward of the right hip. The legs are making the shoulders, arms, hands and club move in one piece, and increasing the tension in the muscles of the back, shoulders, arms and hands as the clubhead is being dragged down. The mental impression is that the hit is with the left thumb which drags the club through the ball. If the right foot is turned insufficiently (less than 10 degrees) to the left at the address, only the right leg, instead of both, will drive and much of the rhythm will be lost.

Fig. 28

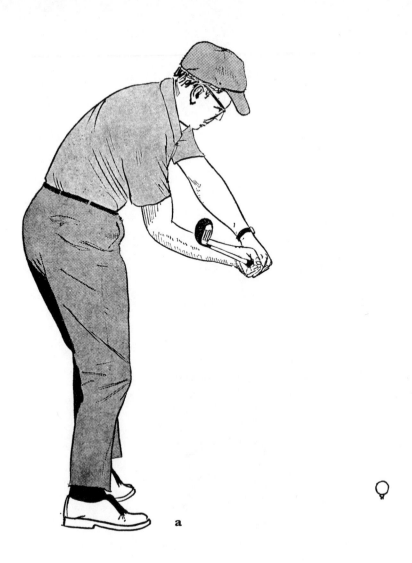

a

Figs. 29a and 29b   The Hitting Area

The club is dragged into the hitting area by the legs. It is the position of the right arm, with the elbow well forward, that makes it possible for the pressure of the legs to be transferred to the club. The right arm is flexed and a considerable amount of energy is being stored up in the extended muscles not only of the arm

b

but of the back and shoulders. As the leg drive continues, the speed of the clubhead is increasing and the muscles of the back, shoulders, arms and hands are being further tensed. The energy is being stored up to be released at impact. It can be seen that the pressure of the legs must build up progressively if the maximum energy is to be stored up in the swing for release during impact. The position of the right elbow is six inches forward of the present accepted position (see Fig. 12), and to achieve this position in the hitting area it has to be well away from the body.

Fig. 30

Fig. 30   The Impact Position

There is no actual hit. The club is dragged through the ball. As the clubhead meets the ball, the shock of impact bends the club shaft and further extends the muscles of the hands, arms, shoulders and back. The legs are still keeping up the pressure. It is the reflex action of the muscles, especially that of the right arm, that keeps up the pressure on the ball that bit longer at impact, giving extra length and control. With a pure reflex hit such as I have described here, the ball is on the clubface for the maximum length of time. This gives "feel", control and good flighting. The clubface is not rolling over. The shot is straight. There is no draw or fade, no hitting from inside to out to counter rolling of the wrists, and the clubface is on the line of flight through the hitting area for the maximum distance. The position of the right elbow, well forward of the right hip, is what this book is all about. It is the only position in which it is possible to make full use of the power of the legs and so hit the ball farther, straighter and with more control.

Fig. 31

Fig. 31   After Impact

The clubface is still square to the direction of travel and has only just come off the line of flight. The clubhead has not passed the hands and there is no rolling over of the wrists. The feet are still firmly on the ground although the outside of the right foot has begun to lift slightly. The head is well back with the right eye coming up under the left. The knees are still bent.

Fig 32.

Fig. 32   The Finish

The hands finish high and the grip has gone back to the address grip. The knees have not straightened and the weight has not shifted. Although the head has turned with the right eye coming up under the left, its position has not altered.

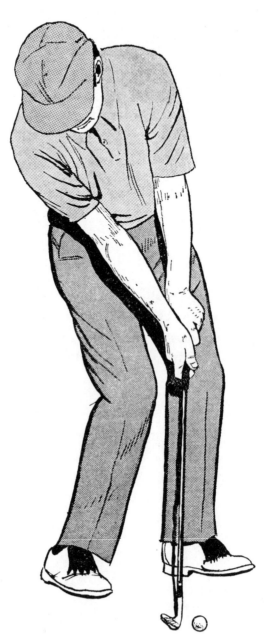

Fig. 33

Fig. 33 The Address

The address is similar to that of the full shot. The left thumb is behind the shaft, the feet are turned towards the target, the elbows are close together and the grip is as for the full shot. The ball is opposite the left heel.

Fig. 34

Fig. 34   The Takeaway

The knees have been pushed towards the hole and held, and the club has been taken back from this forward press. The left wrist has turned under the right, shutting the clubface, and has changed from a concave position to a convex one. The right elbow has hardly moved. The left thumb is still behind the shaft.

Fig. 35

Fig. 35   The Hit

At the top of the swing the legs took over and, by
their forward movement, have dragged the clubhead
through the ball. The hands, wrists and arms were
fully flexed at impact, transmitting the whole weight
of the body. The club is moving slowly but there is
maximum pressure behind the shot. The wrists have
unflexed at impact and given "feel" to the shot. The
left thumb is behind the shot and, as with the full
shot, the "feel" is that the left thumb drags the club
through the ball.

97

Fig. 36

Fig. 36   The Finish

The clubhead has only just caught up with the hands. The head has stayed behind the shot and not moved forward. The clubhead has not rolled over and is still in line with the hole. The right eye is coming up under the left. The "feel" of the chip is that the club is turned under on the backswing and—to use current terminology—the hit is from shut to open.

A repeating swing is extremely difficult to develop and takes many years of trial and practice. For the average golfer the difficulty is to decide what the line of development should be. With the grip, stance, take-away, position of the wrists and so on all to a certain extent inter-related and all tending to vary from day to day, it is not easy to have a steady pro-gramme of development for each part of the swing.

The arc of the club and the position of the hands at the top are the parts of the swing which every-one notices and golf writers discuss. In fact, both are the result of the position of the body and the way in which the swing is started.

I consider that the two most significant points on which the evolution of the swing depends are:

1. Curtailing the hip turn on the backswing,
2. Reducing the amount the left arm has swung around the body on the backswing.

Figs. 37, 38 and 39 illustrate as simply as possible how these two fundamental features of the golf swing are changing as the swing evolves. In the old type of swing the arm is well across the body at the top of the swing in the modern swing it is less so, and in the swing of the future it is nearly at right angles to the chest and almost parallel with the feet. It follows that, in trying to develop or improve his swing, a golfer should concentrate almost entirely on these two features. Other aspects of the swing will then fall into place.

You might ask why I have not mentioned the position of the right elbow in relation to the hip at the hit position. The reason is that I look upon this as the result of having the minimum of hip turn on the backswing and a position at the top of the swing where the arms have hardly come across the body at all. Getting the elbows into a reflex position at the hit so that the legs can be used as the source of power necessitates getting the angle between the left arm and the shoulder as near to a right angle as possible at the top of the swing.

Anyone who is trying to improve their swing should always have these questions of hip turn and the amount the left arm comes across the body in the forefront of their minds. More progress can be made by striving all the time to cut both of them down than by adopting any other aim.

ROUTINE

Every golfer should have a definite routine to position himself accurately in relation to the ball and the target, and to adopt a good posture. It is difficult at any time, and particularly when you are under pressure, to take up a good posture unless you have a very precise routine. Furthermore, when you are under pressure, if you have a reliable routine you will concentrate on this and, as a result, take the tension off yourself.

The routine should not be prolonged but it must be quite definite and it must always be carried out, in practice as well as on the golf course, so that it becomes an integral part of your shot-making. All of the great players have had a clear-cut routine for setting themselves up. There are many possibilities but the one I would suggest is as follows. It is based on the premise that, with the swing I have described, the direction of the shot will be parallel to an imaginary line drawn through the heels.

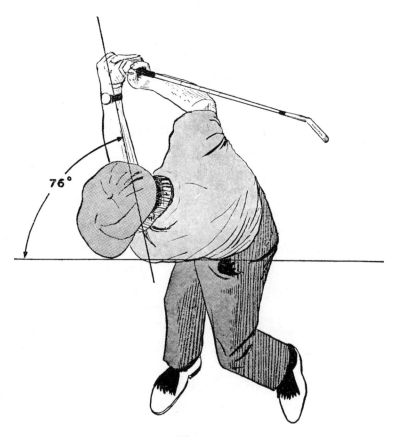

76°

Fig. 37

Fig. 37   Yesterday

Hip turn: 70 degrees; angle between arm and target: 76 degrees. The long, wristy swing is the result of these two basic features. The clubface is open, the left wrist concave. The legs can move independently of the arms.

Fig. 38

Fig. 38   Today

Hip turn: 45 degrees; angle between arm and target: 46 degrees. Less hip turn and a reduction in the amount the arms have gone around the body have resulted in a more compact swing with a square clubface and a flat left wrist. It is a position from which the movement of the arms can be co-ordinated with the legs.

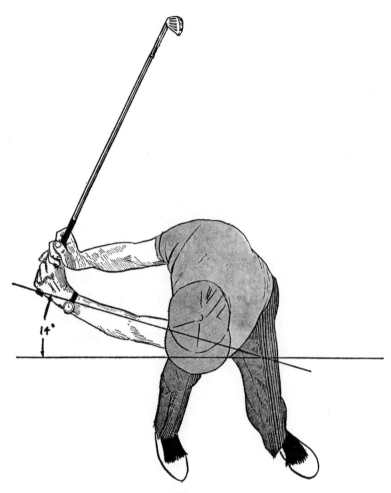

Fig. 39

Fig. 39   Tomorrow

Hip turn: 10 degrees; angle between arm and target: 14 degrees. The minimum of hip turn, combined with a left arm position which has hardly moved across the body at all, has resulted in a more athletic wind-up of the body in which any movement of the legs also moves the arms and club.

When you are addressing the ball it is extremely difficult—in fact, almost impossible—to know where your feet are facing. Therefore, to get a perspective of the shot, you should start behind the ball.

1. Standing a few feet behind the ball, grip the club and do a practice swing or half-swing to make sure that your hands are right.

2. Walk up to the ball from behind, picking a spot 18 inches or so ahead of it and in line with your target.

3. Move to the side and place the clubhead the appropriate distance inside the ball.

4. Stand square to the line of flight—indicated by the ball and the spot you picked 18 inches or so ahead of it—with your feet together. In that position if you look at the hole, turning your head so that your eyes move in the same vertical plane which you follow in executing the shot (that is, with one eye above the other), you can feel that you are lining-up exactly square.

5. Move the left foot one or two inches to the left, turning the toes 30 degrees towards the hole, and move the right foot four, five or six inches to the right, depending on the club you are using. At the same time turn the right foot 10 degrees towards the hole. A line through the heels should be parallel with a line through the ball and the spot you picked ahead of it.

6. Take a last look at where you are aiming, again using the eyes in a vertical plane and making sure that the shoulders remain absolutely square.

7. Raise both sets of toes off the ground to make certain your weight is on your heels.

Then, with a forward press, you're away.

108

PRACTICE

To develop a sound technique, whether it be for playing the piano, hurdling or hitting a golf ball, requires daily practice over many years. The actual technique of playing the piano may seem simple, but to achieve the standard of muscle control which will give you the necessary "feel" represents several hours at the keyboard daily for an extensive period of time. Again, should you decide to write left-handed when you are naturally right-handed, you would know how to hold the pen and what to do with it, but it would take months, or even years, of dedicated practice to become fluent.

In golf the process of practice is further complicated, as has been pointed out earlier in this book, by the uncertainty of knowing what is the best technique to copy. In fact, practice for most golfers means experimenting with their grip, stance, takeaway and so on in an endeavour to recapture a feeling they once experienced when they hit "the perfect shot".

There are so any inter-related parts of the swing—the posture, the grip, the stance—that to get them even remotely co-ordinated while concentrating on making contact with the ball is an almost impossible task. Thus developing a swing is an extremely slow process. To those who do not fully appreciate the extent of the problem the slow progress is frustrating and it is only the very determined who do not give up.

When I took up golf I could see that I should never have the time available to hit sufficient balls to develop and muscle-memorise a sound swing. I tried

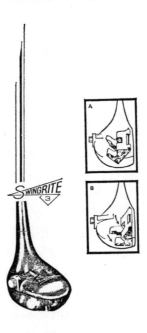

Fig. 40   Swingrite

The Swingrite III (called the 19th Hole Swing Trainer and Exercise Club in the United States) is a practice club which simulates the sound and reaction on the hands ("feel") of a perfect shot. Inside the head is a swing weight and a release mechanism. The swing is started with the swing weight at position A. The adjustable setting on a scale determines the centrifugal force required to operate the release mechanism. When clubhead speed is sufficient to release the mechanism, the swing weight drops down into position B. The centre of gravity of the clubhead has moved out and forward, and the clubhead is slowed down for an instant as is a normal club when it strikes a ball. Swinging this club daily is the best and quickest method of developing a co-ordinated swing.

swinging a club without a ball, but I found this un-satisfactory because you are not bracing against a hit and this method is therefore only an approximation of the real thing and of limited help.

Eventually I made a club in which a weight shifted its position in the clubhead and gave a feeling like cracking a whip. This simulated the sound and impact reaction ("feel") of hitting a ball. The clubhead speed at which this movement took place could be adjusted. With this club I could concentrate on the various parts of the swing and could swing it once every few seconds. I logged up a few hundred thousand swings in quite a short time and had a single-figure handicap within a year.

This club has now been developed commercially and is marketed all over the world. In the United States it is called the 19th Hole Swing Trainer and Exercise Club. In other countries it is marketed under the name of Swingrite (Fig. 40).

I believe that for most golfers the only way to de-velop a sound swing is to use a Swingrite in simulated practice at home where you can concentrate on the details of your swing. Then you can check subse-quently on the practice ground that the swing you are developing actually works. In other words, if you should decide, say, to get your hands higher on the backswing, you would swing a Swingrite in front of a mirror a few thousand times over a week or so until this movement had become instinctive. Then, at the first opportunity, you would try it out on the practice ground. Just getting the hands higher may have al-tered the shoulder turn or some other part of the swing, and you will probably find some other slight modifications are needed. However, by using the Swingrite you can dictate the way your swing de-velops whereas most swings, even those of some professionals, happen by chance after long hours on the practice tee.

You can spend a lifetime improving your swing. Indeed, most professionals do. To get the most out of your golf you should practice 20 to 30 minutes each day so that, over the years, your swing will develop and your game improve. The habit of practising each day is an essential part of maintaining an enthusiasm for the game. It might be argued that it is not in the nature of the average golfer to practise daily. However, sales of the Swingrite, which can now be counted in hundreds of thousands, belie this argument, and those which come back for servicing have, in most cases, been swung hundreds of times daily over a period of years.

I am sure that if the average golfer is prepared to make the effort to set up a comfortable and practical practice area at home, where he can swing a Swingrite in front of a mirror and also practise actual chips and putts, not only will his golf improve over the years but he will be fitter and get more out of the game. You can get out of golf only what you have put into it.

PUTTING

Putting is the most elusive, yet a very important part, of the game of golf. To be a good competitor you have to be a reasonable putter. The proficient putter will always have a different attitude to the game from the poor putter. After a bad shot it is a challenge to the good putter to get a par for he knows that, if he can place his shot to the green reasonably close to the pin, he has a good chance to recover the lost ground. On the other hand, the poor putter usually accepts the loss of a shot and is, of necessity, a defensive player.

Everyone has had days when all the putts go in. The line is easy and the judgement of distance is no trouble. The problem is to make these days more frequent and, in order to achieve this, it is first necessary to analyse what we are trying to do.

There are two aspects of putting: one is the ability to hit the ball on the intended line and the other is to have the touch to hit it the correct strength. The touch is the most important part of putting. In the first place, unless the putt is absolutely straight, the line is entirely dependent on the strength of the putt. Secondly, this feeling for the length of the putt is subconscious and, providing you have it, all your concentration can be applied to the line and your thinking becomes positive.

Hitting the ball on the intended line is a matter of having the head in the right position. I have used the expression "the right eye coming up under the left" several times in this book. In putting this is even more vital. In assessing the line of the putt, the head must turn on a horizontal axis so that both eyes are in the vertical plane which passes through the ball and line of the putt. This position can be clarified in your mind by taking up a stance to putt towards a mirror. As you look up towards the mirror as if to see the line, the reflection of both eyes and the ball should be in the same vertical line. This is probably not necessary for golfers with a strong master eye, but even for them it does help. With most golfers, however, it is possible to see a clear line to the hole only when one eye is above the other in a vertical plane. If they are not, each eye sees a slightly different line.

Hitting the ball an exact distance is a more involved problem. In the first place, the ball must roll from the moment it is struck. It is this rolling movement which keeps the ball on line. It is instinctive for players of billiards or pool to strike the cue ball just above the centre so that it rolls from the moment of impact. In scientific terms, they are applying force through the centre of gyration (Fig. 41a).

The centre of gyration of a golf ball is precisely the same as the centre of gyration of a billiard ball or pool ball. However, most putters have a loft of about 5 degrees so that, if the ball is struck with the shaft vertical and the putter head moving horizontally, the ball will not roll immediately on impact and may even have backspin on it. It will therefore skid for some feet before friction with the grass starts it to roll, and while it is skidding even the slightest imperfections in the putting surface can deflect the ball off line (Fig. 41b).

The problem is how to strike the ball to make it roll from impact. A putter cannot be used to make as precise a striking action as can be achieved with a billiard cue. In an attempt to solve this difficulty I have made various putters with negative loft. I have found that they work for short putts but with longer putts the ball jumps on impact as there is an inclination to drive it into the ground (Fig. 41c).

By trial I have established that the best solution is to hood the club slightly and drag it through the ball (Fig. 41d). By adopting this movement the hands are slightly ahead of the putter so that the putter face becomes vertical. The strike is in the centre of the ball but the line of applied force is through the centre of gyration. This works for all strengths of putts. In fact, most good putters feel that they are dragging the putter through the ball with the back of the left hand which has the effect of hooding the putter face and striking the ball slightly on the upswing.

Being able to roll the ball is the first part of the problem of accurate length. The second, and equally difficult part, is to be able to feel how hard to strike the putt. Again this comes back to application of pressure at impact. It might seem that the ball is on the putter for a very short distance and that the putting stroke is a collision between the ball and the putter head. This is not so. The putt, like other golf shots, should be the application of force through a distance. To get maximum control or "feel" the putter must be swung very slowly with as much pressure as possible behind the shot in order that the flexing of the shaft can keep the ball on the putter blade for as great a distance as possible.

For this reason I believe that the putting stroke should be a miniature of the full swing described in this book, enabling full pressure to be applied at impact and the reflex action of the hands to be used to keep the ball on the putter even longer. Bobby Locke, who must assuredly be the greatest putter of all time, did exactly this.

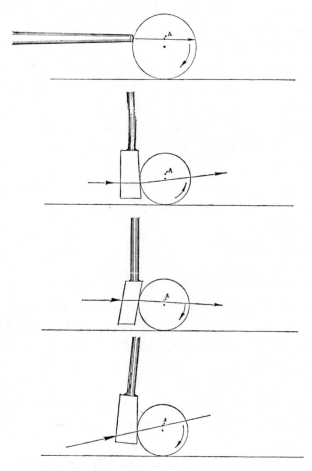

Figs. 41a, b, c, d.

Fig. 41a

The billiard or pool ball is struck just above centre so that it rolls. In scientific terms the force is applied through the centre of gyration (A). A ball which rolls holds its line better and the striker can have more control.

Fig. 41b

The normal putter has a 5-degree loft. Thus, if the shaft is vertical at impact, the ball will most probably have a little backspin and will certainly not roll but will skid for the first few feet.

Fig. 41c

It would seem logical to have a putter with a negative loft to roll the ball. This works for short putts but for longer ones the ball is inclined to jump at impact.

Fig. 41d

To roll the ball with a putter the simplest method is to drag the club through the ball slightly on the upswing so that the resultant force is through the centre of gyration. The hands are a few degrees ahead of the putter blade.

Actual judgement of the length of the putt is relatively easy once you have a repeating firm stroke which rolls the ball. However, there is a psychological aspect to getting the strength right in that "feel" is a subconscious action. In other words, the process of rolling a long putt up to the hole is not one of thinking whether the green is fast or slow, uphill or downhill, but of regarding your subconscious as a computer and, by walking up to the hole and studying the contours and surface of the green, feeding in sufficient information so that the action of taking the putt is technically mechanical but the "feel" is a subconscious action.

Putting and putting under pressure are two entirely different matters. To putt under pressure your method must be very good and there must be no hint of hitting with the hands as the hands are the first part of the body to reflect nervousness. Also, if your method is good both athletically and scientifically, under pressure you will rise to the occasion and putt even better. It is vital to have a definite routine so that you are lined up properly with a positive start to the swing so that it is slow and deliberate.

Golfers are inclined to regard putting as a game within a game. There is no doubt that hours of practice are needed to become proficient either at hitting a ball or at putting, and most golfers have hardly the time to master either. The majority have a very different technique for their long game compared with their putting so that, when their long game is on, their putting tends to be off and vice versa.

This is another reason why I believe the putting method should be a miniature of the full shot. When this is so, every putt should help to make the swing more automatic—the method of taking up the stance, of seeing the line, of starting the swing, and the all-important matter of tempo.

To summarise, the process of taking a putt should be (1) look at the putt from the ball to the hole and the hole to the ball, (2) assess the line and get the feel of the strength of the green, (3) take the same stance as for a full shot but with the feet closer together, (4) before making the stroke look from the ball to the hole with the right eye coming up under the left, (5) start the swing with a slight press of the knees to the hole, hold this position and let the putter swing back slightly hooded. The knees will then automatically drag the putter through the ball. The head remains very still. The hands lead the putter and the strike is slightly on the upswing.

THE GOLF SWING OF THE FUTURE . . .
AND YOU

The theme of this book has been that the two most significant points about the evolution of the golf swing over the years have been (1) the curtailing of hip turn on the backswing, and (2) reduction of the amount the left arm swings around the body on the backswing. These, I believe, signpost the way the swing will continue to evolve in the future, and the swing I have described in these pages does, in fact, take this evolutionary process to its logical conclusion. However, the ordinary club golfer is bound to ask (and quite rightly). "What relevance has this to me?"

Golf, it must be admitted, is not an easy game. To get your handicap down from 10 to 6 requires nearly twice as much effort as getting down to 10 in the first place. To reduce your handicap from 6 to 2 requires four times the effort involved in reducing it from 10 to 6. Then, to progress from a handicap of 2 to being a scratch player requires as much dedication as you have put into your game since you first started.

If one compares golf to the piano, I should say that being able to play at the level of a Nicklaus or a Palmer involves at least as much effort—probably even more—as is needed to turn yourself into a concert pianist. To strike a more optimistic note, however, to be able to play to a handicap of 10 is no more difficult than being able to give a reasonable rendition of *Chopsticks*.

Yet at the present time a handicap of 10, with the vastly increased enjoyment that comes once each shot has ceased to be a great adventure, seems to be beyond the reach of the vast majority of golfers, no matter how keen they may be to improve. I suppose more than 80 per cent of club golfers have handicaps in the "teens" and, even if they buy every instruction book as it comes off the presses and take series of lessons from every pro. within a radius of 10 miles, find themselves unable to make any real progress with their game. Why should this be?

I believe the answer is extremely simple. They cannot achieve a handicap in the region of 10 because they are concentrating on the inessentials of the swing and neglecting the essentials. At the same time they are giving no thought at all to what is the absolute basis of the golf swing—*the posture at the address.*

The foundation of the golf swing—and this cannot be over-stressed—is the ability to take up a posture at the address which allows the shoulders to turn freely on the backswing while the hips turn as little as possible. Almost every known bad shot in golf can be attributed to bad posture at the address. Lifting the head, for instance, is the result of having to pull round with the shoulders because the hips have collapsed on the backswing. Both hitting behind the ball and shanking are caused by not having the weight on the heels at the address.

A further point is that the majority of golfers have not only been playing for years with a faulty foundation to their swing, liable to collapse at any time. They have also been trying to compensate for their bad address position with an equally bad grip or stance. The result is that they can never really hope to improve. On the other hand, if you adopt a good posture at the address, an effective grip is instinctive and there is no problem whatever in taking the club back into a position from which a golf shot can be played with ease.

122

It must be pointed out that there is the finest of lines between a good and a faulty address position. For the low-handicap golfer a good address position is a matter of "feel" and when he hits a bad shot he has almost invariably been slack in setting himself up. The average golfer has never experienced this "feel" and, in his case, a good address position can be assumed consistently only if it is exactly specified.

I am certain that the address position given earlier in this book, with the toes turned towards the target and the shoulders square, works for any swing. It should enable the average golfer to take the club back without the hips collapsing and to get into a position at the top of the swing from which he can hit the ball with ease.

Building up a technique can be done only over a period of time by constant repetition of movements until your muscles behave instinctively as you want them to behave. When you want to change a faulty series of movements which you have made natural to you in the past—i.e. alter your swing—the problem has to be tackled logically and meticulously as it is so easy to slip back into old, familiar habits.

To anyone wishing to adopt the swing outlined in this book, I would say: Tackle it in stages.

Stage 1. Get the posture at the address right. Then concentrate on swinging the club slowly, and as wide as possible, on this firm base you have given yourself. The degree you are restricting your hip turn should be checked regularly in front of a mirror. Once you have made this hip–shoulder relationship instinctive, you should be down to at least a handicap of 10.

Stage 2. Concentrate on the position of the left arm,

gradually restricting the amount it goes round the body on the backswing. By the time this, too, has become instinctive, you should be well down into single figures.

Stage 3. Then—and only then—build in the grip change outlined in Chapter V.

One final word. When you take that last look up the fairway before striking the ball, always be certain that your eyes are in a vertical plane (i.e. one above the other). If your posture, on which all else depends, is not quite perfect, this simple movement will put you back into the right position.

Good golfing!